FORGIVENESS

LIVING
THE GOOD LIFE
TOGETHER

FORGIVENESS
letting go

leader guide

Helen R. Neinast

ABINGDON PRESS / Nashville

LIVING THE GOOD LIFE TOGETHER
FORGIVENESS: LETTING GO
Leader Guide

Copyright © 2006 by Abingdon Press

Scripture quotations in this publication, unless otherwise indicated, are from the New Revised Standard Version of the Bible, copyrighted © 1989 by the Division of Christian Education of the National Council of the Churches of Christ in the United States of America, and are used by permission.

Other quotations are taken from the New King James Version, copyrighted © 1982 by Thomas Nelson, Inc. Used by permission. All rights reserved.

Lectio divina steps adapted by permission from *50 Ways to Pray: Practices From Many Traditions and Times*, by Teresa A. Blythe (Abingdon Press, 2006); pages 45–47.

This book is printed on acid-free, elemental chlorine-free paper.

ISBN 0-687-46600-8

06 07 08 09 10 11 12 13 14 15—10 9 8 7 6 5 4 3 2 1
MANUFACTURED IN THE UNITED STATES OF AMERICA

Contents

SESSION PLANS

ADDITIONAL HELPS

Introduction

LIVING THE GOOD LIFE TOGETHER: A STUDY OF CHRISTIAN CHARACTER IN COMMUNITY

Welcome to Living the Good Life Together! This unique and exciting series is designed to help Christians learn about and put into practice various character traits associated with the Christian faith. Some of these character traits are attentiveness, forgiveness, discernment, intimacy, humility, and hospitality.

Christian life invites us to cultivate habits that continually open us and others to God's grace, a grace that reshapes our desires, thoughts, feelings, and actions. The "good life" in Christ is life shaped by God's grace. When we choose to seek this good life together, we are drawn into the disciplined habits of living as friends of God in the community of others.

Jesus' ministry was spent teaching and showing others God's good life, so much so that he invested extraordinary time and energy with his disciples. In John 1:39, Jesus invited would-be followers to "come and see." This is a response that facilitates learning and understanding. Luke 10:37 offers Jesus' instruction to "go and do likewise," the closing words to the parable of the good Samaritan. With these words, Jesus invites listeners to practice what they have learned about compassion and mercy, to go and do what is neighborly.

Learning about and practicing the character traits of the Christian life can be compared to learning how to play the piano. We must learn basics such as the position of our hands, the scales, how to use the foot pedals, rhythm, melody, and note reading. If we practice, our skill improves. We are able to play music for others as well as for ourselves. And we find joy in the music!

In a similar way, Living the Good Life Together is designed to help us practice being Christian. Each unit is intended to help us understand or learn about an aspect of Christian character, then move into the practice of what we have learned. Together we will explore and practice ways to embody Christian character in community. And we will find joy in the good life!

A billboard or bumper sticker would say it more succinctly: "The Good Life: Get It. Try It. Live It—Together."

FORGIVENESS: LETTING GO

We have been introduced to the study series Living the Good Life Together. Now it is time to turn our attention to the particular trait of Christian character that we will be exploring and focusing upon throughout this study: forgiveness.

Former presidents, great poets, Pulitzer Prize-winning authors and artists, scientists, religious leaders, and behavioral experts—all these have testified to the power and place of forgiveness in human life. Convicted felons, public school teachers, victims of war, and mothers raising children—these, too, know the power and place of forgiveness.

In our war-torn world as well as in the torn places of our own hearts, forgiveness offers a promise of reconciliation and hope. For example, The Forgiveness Project is a national group that counters violence with the practice of forgiveness and conflict resolution. The John Templeton Foundation sponsors forgiveness laboratories to research the effects of forgiveness on the human body and on human relationships. South Africa, with its Truth and Reconciliation Commission, became a laboratory of sorts for the efforts of religious leaders and government politicians to bring about forgiveness and healing.

Jesus' teachings on forgiveness are rich and varied. They are straightforward and direct; but they also bear close study, because some are not what they might seem at first glance. Jesus encouraged forgiveness when he taught about the prodigal son, when he encountered the woman who was about to be stoned for adultery, and when those who were unforgiving and unkind confronted him. Session 2, "The Heart of Christian Living," places forgiveness in the center of our lives as Christians. Session 3, "Crafting Communities of Forgiveness," explores what it means to be a forgiving community. Session 4, "The Dance of Forgiveness," encourages us to practice forgiveness, step by step, in our everyday lives. Session 5, "Challenges to Forgiveness," invites us to persevere in the difficult journey of forgiveness. Session 6, "Planning the Next Steps Together," facilitates the group planning process for putting into practice what members have learned about forgiveness.

Forgiveness is basic to who we are as Christians and to how we live in the world. It is such a powerful force that Reinhold Niebuhr called it "the final possibility of love in history."[1] Because of that—and because forgiveness can sometimes be elusive or misunderstood—the study of forgiveness is an important part of our efforts to live the good life together.

Resource Components

The resources and group sessions in this study function together to foster intimacy with Scripture, with God, and with others. The resources include a study & reflection guide for each participant, a DVD for viewing during group sessions, and this leader guide.

Study & Reflection Guide

The study & reflection guide is designed for use by the group participants. Each person in the group should have his or her own copy. This guide contains the core content of the study. It also contains several important features in addition to the core content.

Psalm for Praying

A psalm appears on the first page of each session. The group will use this psalm as a prayer of invocation at the beginning of the session.

Daily Readings

Scripture readings are included for each day of the week between the group sessions. Participants will read and reflect upon these Scriptures and use the space provided to write notes or questions they would like to bring to the group session. You will also do these daily readings.

Reflections

When introducing core content, space is provided at the bottom of the page for making notes or recording any thoughts brought to mind by the readings.

Faithful Friends

Each participant will be invited to join with one or two others to practice being a faithful friend over the course of the study and beyond. Spaces are provided at the end of Sessions 2–5 in the study & reflection guide where participants can record thoughts, reflections, insights, prayer concerns, or other matters concerning their faithful friends.

DVD

The video segments on the DVD are designed to supplement the core content presented in the study & reflection guide and to inspire and invite the group into the practice of a particular aspect of Christian character. These segments are 6–10 minutes long and will be viewed during the group sessions, as described in this leader guide.

Leader Guide

The leader guide is designed to help you lead your group with confidence and inspiration. It contains all the information you need in order to help your group plan and carry out the study.

Besides introducing the series and the topic of this particular study, the leader guide also provides detailed session plans. These session plans give you easy-to-follow instructions, including what materials you will need and how to prepare the learning area. The plans also encourage you to set aside a time of preparation before the actual session to prepare yourself spiritually and review your approach to the session.

The leader guide introduces you to the unique "Come and See" and "Go and Do" format of the study, including additional helps and examples to use as you implement that format. The leader guide concludes with suggestions for planning a final worship and celebration experience.

STUDY FORMAT

The format of this study series is based on some of Jesus' own words to his followers: "Come and see" (John 1:39), and "Go and do likewise" (Luke 10:37). In each study, the first six sessions are the backbone of the "Come and See" portion. These sessions inspire and teach the group about a particular character trait of the Christian life. The second six sessions are the "Go and Do" portion. For these sessions, the study offers tools to help group members plan how to put into practice what they have learned.

"Come and See"

Session 1: An Introduction to This Study Series

This session is an orientation to the twelve-week study. In the session, group members will learn about the series, the study format, and the particular topic of this study. They will become familiar with the study & reflection guide and learn about the video presentations. They will learn about the term *faithful friends* and about the practice of *lectio divina*.

Sessions 2–5: Topics in Christian Character

These sessions offer information about the aspect of Christian character explored in this particular study. The sessions have a particular format designed to teach participants about that aspect and to foster intimacy with Scripture, with others, and with God.

Session 6: Planning the Next Steps Together

This session facilitates planning for what the group will do together in Sessions 7–12 to practice the Christian character trait they have learned about in the previous sessions. Session 6 in this leader guide, "Planning the Next Steps Together," offers a flexible, step-by-step guide for leading the group through the planning process.

The session builds upon a brainstorming activity that the participants will do before they come together. The participants will write their ideas where prompted in the study & reflection guide before coming to Session 6. Make sure they understand the importance of doing this brainstorming activity ahead of time.

"Go and Do"

Sessions 7–12: Practicing Christian Character

What will the group do?

These "Go and Do" sessions are meant to allow time to live out some of what the group has learned in the "Come and See" portion of the study. The group will put into practice what they planned during Session 6, "Planning the Next Steps Together." The group will also continue the practice of faithful friends throughout this portion of the study.

The group may use these sessions in any number of ways. The idea is to reinforce what they have learned and to deepen their practice of the particular aspect of Christian character. The group might consider planning activities in some of the following categories, which are also given as prompts in the study & reflection guide:

- Lectio divina Scripture passages
- Behavioral changes to make
- Ministry events to consider

- Mission work to conceive and implement
- Speakers to invite
- Field trips, retreats, pilgrimages to take
- Books to read, movies to see

Possibilities for these next sessions can be varied and creative. There are many movies that lend themselves to group study. You could borrow these from your church or a public library or rent them from a video store. Watch these together and discuss. This is a good way to learn more about those in your group as well as about yourself. Is there a book the group could read and discuss together? a series of audio programs? Is there someone in your church or community you would like to invite to share the group's time together? What about additional Bible study? Would each group member want to bring in something—an article, a story, something found on the Internet—for the group to discuss from week to week?

How often will the group meet?

The group will decide how many times and on what dates they will meet. Your group may want to continue meeting weekly, or they may decide meeting dates based upon the types of activities they choose to do. A retreat, for example, may involve an overnight gathering. A mission experience could involve one day or several days. A book study might involve two or more weekly sessions. The point is to plan activities that the group will do together in order to put into practice what they have learned; then, let the content of what you have planned dictate and shape the frequency and format of your meetings.

The final session, which will also be planned by the group, will be a worship and celebration of what the group has learned and practiced during their time together. It will inspire all who have participated in the study to put into everyday life the practices of Christian character they have explored together. It will offer opportunities to express gratitude and commitment to God. (See ideas for this worship and celebration in the "Additional Helps" section on pages 59–63.)

Session Activities

During Sessions 1–6, the "Come and See" portion of the study, you will lead your group through a regular sequence of activities described below. These activities are designed to bring the group together, to create an environment for learning, and to help the group use videos, books, Scripture, and group discussion to explore Christian character. Details of how to prepare for and implement these activities, week by week, are spelled out in this leader guide under "Session Plans" (pages 25–57).

During Sessions 7–12, the "Go and Do" portion of the study, your group will be following its own session plans, but you may want to continue some of the following activities as a part of those sessions.

Welcome

Greet participants, especially members who are new to the study. Remind them to use nametags, and make them feel welcome.

Psalm and Silence

This is a time to center as a group using the psalms provided in the study & reflection guide. For later sessions, you may choose another Scripture passage or reading.

Look and Listen

The group will view the video segments as described in the session plans. For later sessions, your group can use any other materials they choose, such as books, movies, Scripture passages, and group members' experiences.

Reflect and Respond

This is a time to reflect upon and respond to the content of the particular session. Allow for discussion, dialogue, and questions from everyone in the group.

Lectio Divina

The group will experience the ancient practice of prayerfully reading the Scriptures. The practice is described, step by step, in both the study & reflection guide and the leader guide (see as follows on this page and the next).

Pray and Practice

This is a time for closing reflections—about the material, about faithful friend experiences, or about prayer concerns. Close this session with prayer in any way your group wishes.

LECTIO DIVINA

Lectio divina, which means "sacred reading," is sometimes also called "praying the Scriptures." It's an ancient process for engaging the Scriptures in order to hear the voice of God. Sessions 1–5 of the study include lectio divina for a particular Scripture related to the topic of the session. Groups may choose to incorporate the practice of lectio divina in later sessions as well.

The lectio divina process contains the following steps:

Step One: *Silencio*

After everyone has turned to the Scripture, be still. Silently turn all your thoughts and desires over to God. Let go of concerns, worries, or agendas. Just *be* for a few minutes.

Step Two: *Lectio*

Read the passage of Scripture slowly and carefully, either aloud or silently. Reread it. Be alert to any word, phrase, or image that invites you, that puzzles you, that intrigues you. Wait for this word, phrase, or image to come to you; try not to rush it.

Step Three: *Meditatio*

Take the word, phrase, or image from your Scripture passage that comes to you and ruminate over it. Repeat it to yourself. Allow this word, phrase, or image to engage your thoughts, your desires, your memories. Invite anyone who would like to share his or her word, phrase, or image, but don't pressure anyone to speak.

Step Four: *Oratio*

Pray that God transform you through the word, phrase, or image from Scripture. Consider how this word, phrase, or image connects with your life and how God is made known to you in it. This prayer may be either silent or spoken.

Step Five: *Contemplatio*

Rest silently in the presence of God. Move beyond words, phrases, or images. Again, just *be* for a few minutes. Close this time of lectio divina with "Amen."

The preceding steps are also listed in each session plan. Participants will find them in the study & reflection guide on pages 12–13.

FAITHFUL FRIENDS

Each week, pairs or small groups of faithful friends will get together to talk about their experience of practicing the week's discipline. Developing and nurturing faithful friends are important practices that continue throughout the twelve weeks of the study.

The Christian way of life presupposes healthy relationships with God, self, and neighbor in Christ. Learning how to give and to receive the support of a faithful friend is a cornerstone of living the good life together.

The spiritual discipline of faithful friendship may be uncomfortable for some in the group. Some people are quiet and introspective, and the thought of talking about deep, heartfelt issues of Christian faith may feel threatening to them. For this reason, it is important to give a great deal of freedom to the participants in choosing faithful friends and deciding how they wish to support one another during the weeks of the study. The questions listed below can ease faithful friends into conversation in a nonthreatening way.

Faithful friends can stay in touch by e-mail, telephone, or over lunch or coffee. They may think of other ways to stay in touch, such as visiting one another in their homes or enjoying a recreational activity together. In these kinds of activities, encourage participants to take time to talk about the study.

Some faithful friends will appreciate guidance for their conversations together. Encourage them to use the following questions, which are also listed on page 14 in the study & reflection guide.

- How has it gone for you, trying to live the week's practice?
- What's been hard about it?
- What's been easy or comfortable?
- What challenges have there been? What rewards?
- What kinds of things happened this week—at work, at home, in your prayer life—that you want to talk about? Has anything affected your spiritual life and walk?

Faithful friends may meet or communicate as often as they like. The expectation is that they communicate at least once a week. During each session, ask the group as a whole how the practice of faithful friends is going. Ask how they are choosing to communicate. Remind them that faithful friends provide a rewarding way to experience meaningful spiritual growth. Also remind them that they can record any thoughts, reflections, insights, prayer concerns, or other matters concerning their faithful friends in the spaces provided in their study & reflection guide (Sessions 2–5).

Do not ask individual participants to talk about their faithful friends conversations. Doing so may cause embarrassment or unnecessary pressure. As a leader, your comments about the practice of having faithful friends should be supportive and affirming.

If the faithful friends practice doesn't seem to be going well for some of the participants, don't criticize them. Simply suggest a phone call, card, or e-mail saying they are thinking about the faithful friend or praying for them. Every day is a new day that offers many opportunities to support one another. Remind participants to honor confidentiality with their faithful friends, to pray for their faithful friends and for their own role as a faithful friend, to listen deeply to one another, and to demonstrate respect for one another.

How to Organize a Group

Living the Good Life Together is an excellent resource for all people who are looking for meaning in their daily lives, who want to grow in their faith, and who want to practice specific traits of Christian character. Group members may be persons who are not a part of a faith community and yet are seekers on a profound spiritual journey. They may be new Christians or new church members who want to know more about Christian faith. Or they may be people who have been in church a long time but feel a need for spiritual renewal. All such persons desire to engage more deeply with what it means to practice the Christian faith.

In order to start a Living the Good Life Together group, you may want to follow these steps:

1. Read through the leader guide and the study & reflection guide. View all the video segments on the DVD. Think about

the specific character trait dealt with in the study, the issues it generates, and the Scriptures. Prepare to respond to questions that someone may ask about the study.

2. Develop a list of potential group members. An ideal size for a small group is seven to twelve people. Your list should have about twice your target number (fourteen to twenty-four people). Encourage your local church to purchase a copy of the study & reflection guide for each of the persons on your list. This is an invaluable outreach tool.

3. Decide on a location and time for your group.

4. Identify someone who is willing to go with you to visit the persons on your list. Make it your goal to become acquainted with each person you visit. Tell them about Living the Good Life Together. Give them a copy of the study & reflection guide. Even if they choose not to attend the group at this time, they will have an opportunity to study the book on their own. Tell each person the initial meeting time, location, and how many weeks the group will meet. Invite them to become a part of the group. Thank them for their time.

5. Publicize the study through as many channels as are available. Announce it during worship. Print notices in the church newsletter and bulletin and on the church website if you have one. Use free public-event notices in community newspapers. Create fliers for mailing and posting in public places.

6. A few days before the sessions begin, give a friendly phone call or send an e-mail to thank all persons you visited for their consideration and interest. Remind them of the time and location of the first meeting.

How to Lead a Group

The role of the leader is to use the resources and facilitate the group sessions in order to foster intimacy with Scripture, with God, and with others. So what does a leader do?

A Leader Prepares

This leader guide contains specific instructions for planning and implementing the study. Generally speaking, however, a leader has some basic preparation responsibilities. They are:

Pray

Ask for God's guidance as you prepare to lead the session.

Read

Review the session materials and its Scriptures ahead of time. Jot down questions or insights that occur during the reading.

Think About Group Participants

Who are they? What life issues or questions might they have about the theme? about the Scriptures?

Prepare the Learning Area

Gather any needed supplies, such as large sheets of paper, markers, paper and pencils, Bibles, hymn books, audiovisual equipment, masking tape, a Bible dictionary, or Bible commentaries. If you are meeting in a classroom setting, arrange the chairs in a semicircle so that everyone can easily see the video segments that will be shown during the session. Make sure everyone will have a place to sit.

Pray for the Group Participants

Before the participants arrive, pray for each one. Ask for God's blessing on your session. Offer thanks to God for the opportunity to lead the session.

A Leader Creates a Welcoming Atmosphere

Hospitality is a spiritual discipline. A leader helps to create an environment that makes others feel welcome and helps every participant experience the freedom to ask questions and to state opinions. Such an atmosphere is based upon mutual respect.

Greet Participants as They Arrive

Say out loud the name of each participant. If the class is meeting for the first time, use nametags.

Listen

As group discussion unfolds, affirm the comments and ideas of participants. Avoid the temptation to dominate conversation or "correct" the ideas of participants.

Affirm

Thank people for telling about what they think or feel. Acknowledge their contributions to discussion in positive ways, even if you disagree with their ideas.

A Leader Facilitates Discussion

Ask Questions

Use the questions suggested in the session plans or other questions that occur to you as you prepare for the session. Encourage others to ask questions.

Invite Silent Participants to Contribute Ideas

If someone in the group is quiet, you might say something like, "I'm interested in what you're thinking." If participants seem hesitant or shy, do not pressure them to speak. However, do communicate your interest.

Gently Redirect Discussion When Someone in the Group Dominates

You can do this in several ways. Remind the group as a whole that everyone's ideas are important. Invite them to respect one another and to allow others the opportunity to express their ideas. You may establish a group covenant that clarifies such mutual respect. Use structured methods such as going around the circle to allow everyone a chance to speak. Only as a last resort, speak to the person who dominates conversation after the group meeting.

---

1. From *Love and Justice: Selections from the Shorter Writings of Reinhold Niebuhr,* by Reinhold Niebuhr, edited by D. B. Robertson (Westminster/John Knox Press, 1957; page 269).

Session Plans

1. An Introduction to This Study Series

Prepare for the Session

Let your preparation for the session be a time to pay attention to God and to the needs of group members as well as a time to review the content of the session. Find a quiet and comfortable place where you will not be interrupted. Have the DVD, a Bible, and the study & reflection guide available in addition to this leader guide. Have paper and pen available to jot down notes or insights. You may wish to keep these notes in a personal journal during this study.

Pray, asking for God's guidance as you prepare for the session. Read Psalm 103:8, 11-12. Take a moment to reflect upon how this psalm speaks to you.

Review the information about Living the Good Life Together in the introduction to the leader guide to make sure you understand the process for the sessions in the series. Anticipate questions group members might have about the program. Write down any notes and questions you have.

View the video segments "Series Overview" and *"Come and See: Preview."* Write notes and questions suggested by the video segments. If you have time, view all the video segments in the study in order to have a more complete overview.

Read the introduction to the series in the study & reflection guide. Write notes and questions suggested by the material.

Review the information about lectio divina in the introduction to the leader guide (pages 16–17). Read 2 Corinthians 5:16-20 using this process. Write notes or questions that emerge from your reading.

Review the information about faithful friends in the introduction to the leader guide and in the instructions below. Make sure you understand the purpose and process for this practice. Consider ways to support and encourage the process for the group members.

Review the steps in "Lead the Session."

Pray, offering gratitude to God for insights, ideas, and guidance for the session. Give thanks for the group members and for what you will experience together.

Gather Materials and Set Up the Learning Area

- Bibles
- DVD, DVD player, and TV
- Leader guide
- Study & reflection guides, one for each participant
- Nametags and markers or pens
- Chairs in a semicircle for viewing the video

Lead the Session

Welcome (3 minutes)

Greet participants as they arrive. Invite them to make a nametag and to find a place to sit where they can comfortably view the video.

Psalm and Silence (3 minutes)

A psalm for praying appears on the first page of each session of the study & reflection guide. This session is "An Introduction to This Study Series," so participants will not yet have the printed material in front of them for the psalm. Read Psalm 103:8, 11-12 as a prayer of invocation. Follow the praying of the psalm with at least a minute of silence.

Look and Listen (8 minutes)

Introduce the first video segment as follows: "This video presentation offers an overview of our study of Living the Good Life Together. It will invite us to consider the Christian character trait of forgiveness." Then view the video segment "Series Overview."

Reflect and Respond (5 minutes)

Following the video, lead the group in discussing the following questions:

- Whom did you recognize in the photographs at the beginning of the video? What thoughts or feelings did these images evoke for you?
- Learning to play the piano illustrates the need to practice in order to learn a skill. What do you remember about learning a new skill? How does this experience connect to learning to live as a Christian?

Overview of Living the Good Life Together (8 minutes)

Tell About the Study Format

Tell the group members about how Living the Good Life Together will work. The total time for the study is twelve weeks. The structure of the study is based upon Jesus' words to the disciples. The first six sessions, "Come and See," will focus on learning and understanding.

Read aloud John 1:38-39. Tell the group that the "Come and See" part of the study is based upon this Scripture.

The second six sessions, "Go and Do," will focus on application or practice. Read aloud Luke 10:36-37, the end of the parable of the good Samaritan. Tell the group that the "Go and Do" part of the study is based upon this Scripture.

Session 6 of the "Come and See" part will be a group planning time for Sessions 7–12. The group will make plans for "Go and Do" based upon what they have learned in "Come and See." Session 12 will conclude with a worship and celebration for the study on forgiveness.

Tell About the Study & Reflection Guide

Give each participant a study & reflection guide. Tell them to turn to pages 11–12. Together, look at the section describing the study & reflection guide. Read aloud the paragraphs entitled "Psalm for Praying," "Daily Readings," and "Reflections."

Tell About the Video Segments

Tell participants that the group sessions will include a brief video segment designed to inspire and to invite reflection and discussion about forgiveness. The video segments supplement and enhance the core content presented in the study & reflection guide.

Faithful Friends (5 minutes)

Ask the group to look at the section on faithful friends on pages 13–14 of the study & reflection guide. You may say something like the following:

- Pairs or small groups of faithful friends will get together during the week to talk about their experiences with the study. This might be over lunch or coffee, during a walk, or by phone or e-mail.
- Use the following questions to help start your conversation:
  - ✓ How has it gone for you, trying to live the week's practice?
  - ✓ What's been hard about it?
  - ✓ What's been easy or comfortable?
  - ✓ What challenges have there been? What rewards?
  - ✓ What kinds of things happened this week—at work, at home, in your prayer life—that you want to talk about? Has anything affected your spiritual life and walk?
- Ask group members to find a partner or partners. You may ask people to pair up on their own, or you may have people number off to get into pairs. If the group has an odd number of people, ask one group to form as three. Be sure to include yourself in this process of forming faithful friends. Tell the group there will be suggestions at the end of today's session for what they might do this week as faithful friends.

Overview of FORGIVENESS: LETTING GO *(5 minutes)*

Ask participants to look on pages 14–16 in the study & reflection guide at the section called "Forgiveness: Letting Go." Share in your own words the information from the introduction to this leader guide under "Forgiveness: Letting Go" (pages 8–9). Emphasize the following points from this material:

- People from all walks of life have testified to the power and place of forgiveness in human life.

29

- In our war-torn world as well as in the torn places of our own hearts, forgiveness offers a promise of reconciliation and hope.
- Jesus' teachings on forgiveness are rich and varied. They are straightforward and direct; yet they bear close study, because some are rich in their complexity.
- Jesus and the prodigal son, Jesus and the woman caught in adultery—Scripture tells story after story about forgiveness and God's grace.
- This study relies on the idea that forgiving and being forgiven are critical parts of our life in the faith. Session 2, "The Heart of Christian Living," places forgiveness in the center of our lives as Christians. Session 3, "Crafting Communities of Forgiveness," explores what it means to be a forgiving community. Session 4, "The Dance of Forgiveness," encourages us to practice forgiveness, step by step, in our everyday lives. Session 5, "Challenges to Forgiveness," invites us to persevere in the difficult journey of forgiveness. Session 6, "Planning the Next Steps Together," facilitates the group planning process for putting into practice what members have learned about forgiveness.
- Forgiveness is basic to who we are as Christians and to how we live in the world.

Lectio Divina (10 minutes)

For this introductory session, the group will not have read any Bible passages or chapter content. Have someone read aloud 2 Corinthians 5:16-20, the story of the lilies of the field. Ask what this Scripture means in light of the theme of forgiveness.

Tell the group that they will use the ancient practice of lectio divina to prayerfully engage 2 Corinthians 5:16-20. As a group, use the lectio divina approach outlined as follows to pray this Scripture.

Step One: *Silencio*

After everyone has turned to the Scripture, be still. Silently turn all your thoughts and desires over to God. Let go of concerns, worries, or agendas. Just *be* for a few minutes.

Step Two: *Lectio*

Read the passage of Scripture slowly and carefully, either aloud or silently. Reread it. Be alert to any word, phrase, or image that invites you, that puzzles you, that intrigues you. Wait for this word, phrase, or image to come to you; try not to rush it.

Step Three: *Meditatio*

Take the word, phrase, or image from your Scripture passage that comes to you and ruminate over it. Repeat it to yourself. Allow this word, phrase, or image to engage your thoughts, your desires, your memories. Invite anyone who would like to share his or her word, phrase, or image, but don't pressure anyone to speak.

Step Four: *Oratio*

Pray that God transform you through the word, phrase, or image from Scripture. Consider how this word, phrase, or image connects with your life and how God is made known to you in it. This prayer may be either silent or spoken.

Step Five: *Contemplatio*

Rest silently in the presence of God. Move beyond words, phrases, or images. Again, just *be* for a few minutes. Close this time of lectio divina with "Amen."

Look and Listen (6 minutes)

Introduce the second video segment as follows: "This video presentation offers a preview of our study of forgiveness. It will invite us to consider the spiritual discipline of forgiveness in the context

31

of our sometimes unforgiving culture." Then view the video segment "*Come and See.* Preview."

Pray and Practice (5 minutes)

This Week's Practice

Encourage group members to do the following:

- Contact their faithful friend this week for coffee, lunch, a walk, or a phone conversation, and talk with that friend about her or his experience of practicing forgiveness this week. Remind the friend to use the list of questions in the "Faithful Friends" section of Session 1, "An Introduction to This Study Series," in the study & reflection guide (pages 13–14).
- Do the daily readings listed in Session 2: "The Heart of Christian Living," in the study & reflection guide (pages 18–19).
- In the study & reflection guide, review Session 1, "An Introduction to This Study Series." Then read Session 2, "The Heart of Christian Living" (pages 17–28). Write notes or questions for discussion in the reflections space.

Closing Prayer

- Share prayer concerns.
- Invite participants to pray for their faithful friend and for the group this week.
- Imagine and discuss possible steps that group members might take this week to put into practice the week's learnings.

Close with a prayer asking God to support each participant. Pray that group members will sense God's support and the encouragement of the group as they seek ways to practice forgiveness during the weeks ahead.

2. THE HEART OF CHRISTIAN LIVING

Prepare for the Session

Let your preparation for the session be a time to pay attention to God and to the needs of group members as well as a time to review the content of the session. Find a quiet and comfortable place where you will not be interrupted. Have the DVD, a Bible, and the study & reflection guide available in addition to this leader guide. Have paper and pen available to jot down notes or insights.

Pray, asking God's guidance as you prepare for the session. Read Psalm 139:23-24 prayerfully.

View the video segment "The Heart of Christian Living." Write notes and questions suggested by the video.

Read Session 2, "The Heart of Christian Living," in the study & reflection guide and the Scriptures mentioned in the daily readings and text. Write notes and questions suggested by the material.

Review the description of lectio divina in the introduction to this leader guide (pages 16–17). Read Luke 15:11–32 (prodigal son) using this process. Write notes or questions that emerge from your reading.

Review the steps in "Lead the Session."

Pray, offering gratitude to God for insights, ideas, and guidance during the session. Thank God for the group members and for what you will experience together.

Gather Materials and Set Up the Learning Area

- Bibles
- DVD, DVD player, and TV
- Leader guide
- Study & reflection guide, one for each participant (participants may bring their own copies)
- Nametags and markers or pens
- Chairs in a semicircle for viewing the video

Lead the Session

Welcome (5 minutes)

Greet participants as they arrive. Invite them to take a name-tag and find a place to sit where they can comfortably view the video.

Psalm and Silence (3 minutes)

Read Psalm 139:23-24 as a prayer of invocation. Follow the praying of the psalm with at least a minute of silence.

Look and Listen (10 minutes)

Introduce the video segment as follows: "This video presentation invites us to consider forgiveness as the heart of Christian living." Then view the video segment, "The Heart of Christian Living."

Reflect and Respond (25 minutes)

Following the video segment, lead the group in discussing these questions:

- Which part of this video spoke most strongly to you? Why?
- In the story of the prodigal son, which character did you relate most strongly to? Why?
- Which do you think is more difficult: forgiving or accepting forgiveness? What did you learn about forgiveness from watching the video?

Invite participants to recall the daily readings in the Bible done in preparation for the group meeting. Ask:

- What did the Scriptures say to you about forgiveness?

• What did the Scriptures say to you about forgiveness being the "heart of Christian living"?

Invite participants to recall their reading this week in Session 2 of the study & reflection guide. Ask:

- What thoughts or questions did you write in the spaces for reflection?
- How do you respond to the statement, "Our ability to experience joy is discovered in our capacity to forgive"?
- What difficult issues do you face right now when it comes to forgiving and being forgiven?
- Broken promises, the inability or unwillingness to believe God forgives us, the trial of trying to forgive someone we really do not want to forgive—which of these cause you to struggle? Why?
- How do you respond to the statement, "Christian forgiveness—and, more specifically, forgiven-ness—is a way of life, a faithfulness that must be learned and relearned"?

Lectio Divina (10 minutes)

As a group, use the approach outlined as follows to pray this Scripture: Luke 15:11-32.

Step One: *Silencio*

After everyone has turned to the Scripture, be still. Silently turn all your thoughts and desires over to God. Let go of concerns, worries, or agendas. Just *be* for a few minutes.

Step Two: *Lectio*

Read the passage of Scripture slowly and carefully, either aloud or silently. Reread it. Be alert to any word, phrase, or image that invites you, that puzzles you, that intrigues you. Wait for this word, phrase, or image to come to you; try not to rush it.

Step Three: *Meditatio*

Take the word, phrase, or image from your Scripture passage that comes to you and ruminate over it. Repeat it to yourself. Allow this word, phrase, or image to engage your thoughts, your desires, your memories. Invite anyone who would like to share his or her word, phrase, or image, but do not pressure anyone to speak.

Step Four: *Oratio*

Pray that God transform you through the word, phrase, or image from Scripture. Consider how this word, phrase, or image connects with your life and how God is made known to you in it. This prayer may be either silent or spoken.

Step Five: *Contemplatio*

Rest silently in the presence of God. Move beyond words, phrases, or images. Again, just *be* for a few minutes. Close this time of lectio divina with "Amen."

Pray and Practice (5 minutes)

This Week's Practice

Encourage group members to do the following:

- Contact their faithful friend this week and talk with that friend about his or her experience of the practice of forgiveness. Remind them to use the list of questions in the "Faithful Friends" section of Session 1, "An Introduction to This Study Series," in the study & reflection guide (pages 13–14).
- Do the daily readings listed in Session 3, "Crafting Communities of Forgiveness," in the study & reflection guide (pages 30–31).
- Read Session 3, "Crafting Communities of Forgiveness," in the study & reflection guide (pages 29–38). Write notes or questions for reflection or discussion in the reflections space.

Closing Prayer

- Share prayer concerns.
- Invite participants to pray this week for their faithful friend and for the group.
- Imagine and discuss possible steps that group members might take to put into practice the week's learnings about seeing forgiveness at the heart of Christian living.

Close with a prayer asking God to support each participant. Pray that group members will sense God's support and the encouragement of the group as they seek ways this week to forgive and to be forgiven.

3. CRAFTING COMMUNITIES OF FORGIVENESS

Prepare for the Session

Let your preparation for the session be a time to pay attention to God and to the needs of group members as well as a time to review the content of the session. Find a quiet and comfortable place where you will not be interrupted. Have the DVD, a Bible, and the study & reflection guide available in addition to this leader guide. Have paper and pen available to jot down notes or insights.

Pray, asking God's guidance as you prepare for the session. Read prayerfully Psalm 32:3-5.

View the video segment "Crafting Communities of Forgiveness." Write notes and questions suggested by the video.

Read Session 3, "Crafting Communities of Forgiveness," in the study & reflection guide and the Scriptures mentioned in the daily readings and text. Write notes and questions suggested by the material.

Review the description of lectio divina in the introduction to this leader guide (pages 16–17). Read Matthew 18:21-35 using this process. Write notes or questions that emerge from your reading.

Review the steps in "Lead the Session."

Pray, offering gratitude to God for insights, ideas, and guidance for the session. Thank God for the group members and for what you will experience together.

Gather Materials and Set Up the Learning Area

- Bibles
- DVD, DVD player, and TV
- Leader guide
- Study & reflection guide, one for each participant (participants may bring their own copies)
- Nametags and markers or pens
- Chairs in a semicircle for viewing the video

Lead the Session

Welcome (5 minutes)

Greet participants as they arrive. Invite them to take a name-tag and to find a place to sit where they can comfortably view the video.

Psalm and Silence (3 minutes)

Read Psalm 32:3-5 as a prayer of invocation. Follow the praying of the psalm with at least a minute of silence.

Look and Listen (10 minutes)

Introduce the video segment as follows: "This video presentation offers reflections on the importance of communities of forgiveness." Then view the video segment, "Crafting Communities of Forgiveness."

Reflect and Respond (25 minutes)

Following the video, lead the group in discussing these questions:

- What thoughts or feelings emerged for you as you watched the video segment?
- What did you learn about South Africa's Truth and Reconciliation process? What applications of that process can you see in your own life?
- Peter Storey talks about corporate sin (group sin) and how easy it is to overlook. What are some examples of corporate sin in our own lives?

Invite participants to recall the daily readings in the Bible that were done in preparation for the group meeting. Ask:

- What did the Scriptures say to you about forgiveness?
- How did the Scriptures speak to you about being part of a community of forgiveness?

Invite participants to recall the session material they read for this week. Ask:

- What thoughts or questions did you write in the reflection spaces?
- Look at the statements about sin as what we do or fail to do in the study and reflection guide, page 33. How do you understand sin? How do you see the connections among sin, forgiveness, and helping to create communities of forgiveness?
- What does the statement, "Christian practices must be bound up with the support and challenge of friends," suggest to you?

Lectio Divina (10 minutes)

As a group, use the approach outlined as follows to pray this Scripture: Matthew 18:21-35.

Step One: *Silencio*

After everyone has turned to the Scripture, be still. Silently turn all your thoughts and desires over to God. Let go of concerns, worries, or agendas. Just *be* for a few minutes.

Step Two: *Lectio*

Read the passage of Scripture slowly and carefully, either aloud or silently. Reread it. Be alert to any word, phrase, or image that invites you, that puzzles you, that intrigues you. Wait for this word, phrase, or image to come to you; try not to rush it.

Step Three: *Meditatio*

Take the word, phrase, or image from your Scripture passage that comes to you and ruminate over it. Repeat it to yourself. Allow this word, phrase, or image to engage your thoughts, your desires, your memories. Invite anyone who would like to share his or her word, phrase, or image, but do not pressure anyone to speak.

Step Four: *Oratio*

Pray that God transform you through the word, phrase, or image from Scripture. Consider how this word, phrase, or image connects with your life and how God is made known to you in it. This prayer may be either silent or spoken.

Step Five: *Contemplatio*

Rest silently in the presence of God. Move beyond words, phrases, or images. Again, just *be* for a few minutes. Close this time of lectio divina with "Amen."

Pray and Practice (5 minutes)

This Week's Practice

Encourage group members to do the following:
- Contact their faithful friend this week. Ask them to talk with their faithful friend about forgiveness and being forgiven in light of Paul's advice to "speak the truth" (Ephesians 4:25). Remind them to use the list of questions in the "Faithful Friends" section of Session 1, "An Introduction to This Study Series," in the study & reflection guide (pages 13–14).
- Do the daily readings listed in Session 4, "The Dance of Forgiveness," in the study & reflection guide (pages 40–41).
- Read Session 4, "The Dance of Forgiveness," in the study & reflection guide (pages 39–48). Write notes or questions for reflection or discussion in the reflections space.

Closing Prayer

- Share prayer concerns.

- Invite participants to pray for their faithful friend and for the group this week.
- Imagine and discuss possible steps that group members might take to put into practice the week's learnings about communities of forgiveness.

Close with a prayer asking God to support each participant. Pray that group members will gain a sense of how to live their daily lives in a way that will help to create a community of forgiveness.

4. THE DANCE OF FORGIVENESS

Prepare for the Session

Let your preparation for the session be a time to pay attention to God and to the needs of group members as well as a time to review the content of the session. Find a quiet and comfortable place where you will not be interrupted. Have the DVD, a Bible, and the study & reflection guide available in addition to this leader guide. Have paper and pen available to jot down notes or insights.

Pray, asking God's guidance as you prepare for the session. Read Psalm 26:1-3 prayerfully.

View the video segment "The Dance of Forgiveness." Write notes and questions suggested by the video.

Read Session 4, "The Dance of Forgiveness," in the study & reflection guide as well as the Scriptures mentioned in the daily readings and text. Write notes and questions suggested by the material.

Review the description of lectio divina in the introduction to this leader guide (pages 16–17). Read Matthew 7:1-5 using this process. Write notes or questions that emerge from your reading.

Review the steps in "Lead the Session."

Pray, offering gratitude to God for insights, ideas, and guidance for the session. Thank God for the group members and for what you will experience together.

Gather Materials and Set Up the Learning Area

- Bibles
- DVD, DVD player, and TV
- Leader guide
- Study & reflection guide, one for each participant (participants may bring their own copies)
- Nametags and markers or pens
- Chairs in a semicircle for viewing the video

Lead the Session

Welcome (5 minutes)

Greet participants as they arrive. Invite them to take a name-tag and to find a place to sit where they can comfortably view the video.

Psalm and Silence (3 minutes)

Read Psalm 26:1-3 as a prayer of invocation. Follow the praying of the psalm with at least a minute of silence.

Look and Listen (10 minutes)

Introduce the video segment as follows: "This video presentation offers insights that help us understand that forgiveness is a process, a dance, something that happens one step at a time." Then view the video segment "The Dance of Forgiveness."

Reflect and Respond (25 minutes)

Following the video, lead the group in discussing these questions:

- Which part of this video spoke most strongly to you? Why?
- Forgiveness and reconciliation are a process that begins with truth telling, leads to change, and generates a forward-looking yearning for reconciliation. What has been your experience with the first "step" in the dance of forgiveness—telling the truth?
- Of the six steps outlined in the video, which do you find most challenging?
- The two women in the video talk about the "ebb and flow" of their friendship, the tenacity of their commitment to one another, and the compassion they feel toward each other. How

did you react to their story? What can you learn from their reflections?

- The passage in Romans describes all of creation as waiting on tiptoe for the kingdom of God to be revealed. How does your life as a Christian fit with this vision of being on tiptoe in anticipation of forgiveness and grace?

Invite the participants to recall the daily readings in the Bible done in preparation for the group meeting. Ask:

- What did the Scriptures say to you about the dance of forgiveness?
- How did the Scriptures speak to you about forgiveness?
- What connections do you see between the Scriptures and the steps in the dance of forgiveness?

Invite participants to recall the session material they read for this week. Ask:

- What thoughts or questions did you write in the reflection spaces?
- What connections do you make between forgiveness and Tertullian's idea of patience as "the mother of mercy"?
- How do you understand the statement: "Christians can live into the patterns of forgiveness offered by Christ if we begin to learn the steps of a beautiful, if sometimes awkward, dance of forgiveness"?
- Ephesians 4:26 says, "Be angry but do not sin." How do you understand that advice? Can you recall a time when you were angry and still able to use that anger as a source of energy rather than as a source of destruction? What is your response to Buechner's remarks about anger? (pages 42–43)
- What does "changing the conditions that perpetuate our conflicts" suggest to you?

Lectio Divina (10 minutes)

As a group, use the approach outlined as follows to pray this Scripture: Matthew 7:1-5.

Step One: *Silencio*

After everyone has turned to the Scripture, be still. Silently turn all your thoughts and desires over to God. Let go of concerns, worries, or agendas. Just *be* for a few minutes.

Step Two: *Lectio*

Read the passage of Scripture slowly and carefully, either aloud or silently. Reread it. Be alert to any word, phrase, or image that invites you, that puzzles you, that intrigues you. Wait for this word, phrase, or image to come to you; try not to rush it.

Step Three: *Meditatio*

Take the word, phrase, or image from your Scripture passage that comes to you and ruminate over it. Repeat it to yourself. Allow this word, phrase, or image to engage your thoughts, your desires, your memories. Invite anyone who would like to share his or her word, phrase, or image, but do not pressure anyone to speak.

Step Four: *Oratio*

Pray that God transform you through the word, phrase, or image from Scripture. Consider how this word, phrase, or image connects with your life and how God is made known to you in it. This prayer may be either silent or spoken.

Step Five: *Contemplatio*

Rest silently in the presence of God. Move beyond words, phrases, or images. Again, just *be* for a few minutes. Close this time of lectio divina with "Amen."

Pray and Practice (5 minutes)

This Week's Practice

Encourage group members to do the following:

- Contact their faithful friend this week. Invite them to talk about forgiveness in light of viewing one another as beloved children of God (Ephesians 5:1-2). Remind them to use the list of questions in the "Faithful Friends" section of Session 1, "An Introduction to This Study Series," in the study & reflection guide (pages 13–14).
- Do the daily readings listed in Session 5, "Challenges to Forgiveness," in the study & reflection guide (pages 00).
- Read Session 5, "Challenges to Forgiveness," in the study & reflection guide (pages 49–58). Write notes or questions for reflection or discussion in the reflections space.

Closing Prayer

- Share prayer concerns.
- Invite participants to pray for their faithful friend and for the group this week.
- Imagine and discuss possible steps that group members might take to put into practice what they have learned this week about the dance of forgiveness.

Close with a prayer asking God to support each participant. Pray that each participant will be encouraged to spend time listening to God's desires for their life and that they will understand themselves as being deeply forgiven and loved by God. Pray for God's guidance on what steps in the dance of forgiveness might look like for them.

5. CHALLENGES TO FORGIVENESS

Prepare for the Session

Let your preparation for the session be a time to pay attention to God and to the needs of group members as well as a time to review the content of the session. Find a quiet and comfortable place where you will not be interrupted. Have the DVD, a Bible, and the study & reflection guide available in addition to this leader guide. Have paper and pen available to jot down notes or insights.

Pray, asking God's guidance as you prepare for the session. Read Psalm 25:6-7 prayerfully.

View the video segment "Challenges to Forgiveness." Write notes and questions suggested by the video.

Read Session 5, "Challenges to Forgiveness," in the study & reflection guide, as well as the Scriptures mentioned in the daily readings and text. Write notes and questions suggested by the material.

Review the description of lectio divina in the introduction to this leader guide (pages 16–17). Read Luke 6:27-31 using this process. Write notes or questions that emerge from your reading.

Review the steps in "Lead the Session."

Pray, offering gratitude to God for insights, ideas, and guidance for the session. Thank God for the group members and for what you will experience together.

Gather Materials and Set Up the Learning Area

- Bibles
- DVD, DVD player, and TV
- Leader guide
- Study & reflection guide, one for each participant (participants may bring their own copies)
- Nametags and markers or pens
- Chairs in a semicircle for viewing the video

Lead the Session

Welcome (5 minutes)

Greet participants as they arrive. Invite them to take a name-tag and to find a place to sit where they can comfortably view the video.

Psalm and Silence (3 minutes)

Read Psalm 25:6-7 as a prayer of invocation. Follow the praying of the psalm with at least a minute of silence.

Look and Listen (10 minutes)

Introduce the video segment as follows: "This video presentation offers ideas about forgiveness and some of the challenges to forgiveness." Then view the video segment "Challenges to Forgiveness"

Reflect and Respond (25 minutes)

Following the video, lead the group in discussing these questions:

- What thoughts or feelings emerged for you as you watched the video?
- Michael Williams says that the lawyer, even after he heard Jesus' story about the Samaritan, could not quite bring himself to speak the word *Samaritan*. Instead, he answered Jesus' question by saying, "The one who showed him mercy." Have you witnessed that kind of animosity before? How does it feel to come across this kind of prejudice and fear?
- How does understanding the image of God in others affect how you live?
- Nelson Johnson talks about trying to love people who are violently opposed to you. He says any chance he has of doing so is

rooted in his belief that the same God who loves him also loves these enemies. What do you think about that idea?

• Johnson says that yesterday cannot be changed, but there is a tomorrow in which we can strive to do something new, something different. He hopes for a world in which there is "more generosity, more justice, more respect." How do you see God in Johnson's journey—the early racism in his life, his being shot, his friends killed by the Klan—how do you see God in his journey?

• Johnson is clear that his ability to forgive is centered in his deep realization that God loves him. Why do you think he believes that?

• How did the video segment help you to think about your personal struggles with forgiveness? about any specific challenges your faith community faces?

Invite participants to recall the daily readings in the Bible that were done in preparation for the group meeting. Ask:

• What did the Scriptures say to you about forgiveness?
• How did the Scriptures speak to you about challenges to forgiveness?

Invite participants to recall the session material they read for this week. Ask:

• What thoughts or questions did you write in the reflection spaces?
• The session material asks "Don't we usually build walls around us because of insecurity?" How do you respond to this question? What walls do you see in our world? in our communities? in the relationships of your daily lives? How could these walls become bridges?
• What is your response to the statement, "We can't allow even legitimate boundaries to become impenetrable barriers"? What does this statement say to you about risk? about hope? about the challenges of forgiveness?

Lectio Divina (10 minutes)

As a group, use the approach outlined as follows to pray this Scripture: Luke 6:27-31.

Step One: Silencio

After everyone has turned to the Scripture, be still. Silently turn all your thoughts and desires over to God. Let go of concerns, worries, or agendas. Just *be* for a few minutes.

Step Two: Lectio

Read the passage of Scripture slowly and carefully, either aloud or silently. Reread it. Be alert to any word, phrase, or image that invites you, that puzzles you, that intrigues you. Wait for this word, phrase, or image to come to you; try not to rush it.

Step Three: Meditatio

Take the word, phrase, or image from your Scripture passage that comes to you and ruminate over it. Repeat it to yourself. Allow this word, phrase, or image to engage your thoughts, your desires, your memories. Invite anyone who would like to share his or her word, phrase, or image, but don't pressure anyone to speak.

Step Four: Oratio

Pray that God transform you through the word, phrase, or image from Scripture. Consider how this word, phrase, or image connects with your life and how God is made known to you in it. This prayer may be either silent or spoken.

Step Five: Contemplatio

Rest silently in the presence of God. Move beyond words, phrases, or images. Again, just *be* for a few minutes. Close this time of lectio divina with "Amen."

Pray and Practice (5 minutes)

This Week's Practice

Encourage group members to do the following:

- Contact their faithful friend this week. Ask them to talk with that friend as a resource to strengthen their connection with God. Remind them to use the list of questions in the "Faithful Friends" section of Session 1, "An Introduction to This Study Series," in the study & reflection guide (pages 13–14).
- Read Session 6, "Planning the Next Steps Together," in the study & reflection guide (pages 59–63). Write ideas in the boxes provided (pages 62–63). Remind the group that Session 6 is a planning session for what the group will do together for the second phase of the study, "Go and Do." The success of Session 6 will depend upon each member of the group brainstorming ideas during the coming week in preparation for the group meeting.
- Continue the practice of lectio divina on their own and with others.

Closing Prayer

- Share prayer concerns.
- Invite participants to pray for their faithful friend and for the group this week.
- Imagine and discuss possible steps that group members might take to put into practice the week's learnings about challenges to forgiveness.

Close with a prayer asking God to support each participant. Pray that group members will be encouraged to pray for ways to address the challenges of forgiveness in their own lives. Pray for the work group members will do to prepare for the "Go and Do" part of this study on forgiveness.

6. Planning the Next Steps Together

Prepare for the Session

Let your preparation for the session be a time to pay attention to God and to the needs of group members as well as a time to review the content of the session. Find a quiet and comfortable place where you will not be interrupted. Have the DVD, a Bible, and the study & reflection guide available in addition to this leader guide. Have paper and pen available to jot down notes or insights.

Pray, asking God's guidance as you prepare for the session. Read Psalm 139:23-24 prayerfully.

Review the information about "Go and Do" in the introduction to this leader guide (pages 13–15) to make sure you understand the planning process for the remaining six sessions. Anticipate questions the group members might have about the program. Write notes and questions you have.

Read Session 6, "Planning the Next Steps Together," in the study & reflection guide (pages 59–63). Write notes and questions suggested by the material. Brainstorm ideas for what you might do as a group over the next six weeks using the idea prompts at the end of the study & reflection guide (pages 62–63).

View the video segment "*Go and Do:* Review and a Challenge." Write notes and questions suggested by the video.

Review the steps in "Lead the Session."

Pray, offering gratitude to God for insights, ideas, and guidance for the session. Thank God for the group members and for what you will experience together.

Gather Materials and Set Up the Learning Area

- Bibles
- DVD, DVD player, and TV
- Leader guide
- Study & reflection guide, one for each participant (participants may bring their own copies)

- Nametags and markers or pens
- Whiteboard and markers, chalkboard and chalk, or a large sheet of paper and markers
- Masking tape
- Pens or pencils
- Chairs arranged in a semicircle for viewing the video

Lead the Session

Welcome (3 minutes)

Greet participants as they arrive. Invite them to find a place to sit where they can comfortably view the video.

Psalm and Silence (5 minutes)

Read Psalm 139:23-24 as a prayer of invocation. Follow the praying of the psalm with at least a minute of silence.

Look and Listen (8 minutes)

Introduce the video segment as follows: "This video presentation offers a review of what we have studied in the 'Come and See' portion of our study. It also offers a challenge to practice what we have learned." View the video segment "*Go and Do*: Review and a Challenge."

Reflect and Respond (5 minutes)

Ask the following questions to stimulate discussion:

- How do you understand the challenge presented in the video segment?
- What learnings did you write about in your study & reflection guide as you prepared for today's session? What connections

do you see between your learnings and the review of highlights presented in the video segment?

Plan Together (30 minutes)

Say: "During this session, we will plan together how we as a group will put into practice what we have learned about forgiveness. Our plan should reinforce what we have learned, set up future meetings so we can practice what we have learned, learn more through our practice, and deepen our practice of being a faithful friend. We can use our next six weeks in many ways. We are the ones who will decide what we will do and when we will meet."

Explore Together

Discuss which aspects of the study of forgiveness your group wants to explore in the weeks ahead: forgiveness as the heart of Christian living, crafting communities of forgiveness, the dance of forgiveness, and challenges to forgiveness. It is not necessary to choose one session only, but it may be helpful to learn which sessions had the most meaning for the group so that they might explore those topics more in-depth. Use this discussion as a way of working through a list of ideas.

List and Select Ideas

Invite the group to say what ideas they brainstormed and wrote in the boxes provided in Session 6 of their study & reflection guide (pages 62–63). Create a master list of their suggestions on a large sheet of paper, a chalkboard, or a whiteboard using the same idea prompts found in the boxes in the study & reflection guide. After you have listed all the group's ideas, give participants a marker and invite them to make a checkmark beside the five they like best. Ask them to consider the ideas in light of their discussion on the most meaningful topics. List the ones that receive the most checkmarks. If you have more than five in the list, continue the process until it has been reduced to five ideas. You will use this list as a source for scheduling the next six weeks. *Be sure to include a closing worship and celebration for the final session.* (See ideas for this concluding worship and celebration in the "Additional Helps" section on pages 59–63 in this leader guide.)

Create a Schedule

Decide how many times and on what dates you will meet over the next six weeks. Some of your ideas may require meeting weekly. Other ideas may require another schedule. Meeting dates will be based upon the types of activities you choose to do. For example, a retreat may involve an overnight gathering. A mission experience could involve one day or several days. A book study might involve two or more weekly sessions. The point is to plan activities that you will do together in order to put into practice what you have learned. The schedule will emerge from the activities that you choose. Whatever your schedule, decide on dates and times. Record your plan on a calendar. Make sure that group members understand the meeting commitments they are making.

Designate Tasks

Will you need to make arrangements for speakers? Will you need to gather materials such as books, DVDs, or other resources? Will you need to make arrangements for a retreat or a field trip? Who will do such tasks? Who will be willing to serve on a worship and celebration team for the final meeting together? Make these decisions as a group and record them. Again, make sure that group members understand the commitments they are making.

Pray and Practice (5 minutes)

Practice for the "Go and Do" Portion of the Study

Thank the group for what they have contributed to the planning process for the weeks ahead. Encourage group members to do the following:

- Contact their faithful friend each week for coffee, lunch, a walk, or a phone conversation during the "Go and Do" portion of the study.
- Talk together about the plans the group has made and about the various activities they will experience as a group.
- Continue to use the questions in the "Faithful Friends" material in Session 1 of their study & reflection guide, "An Introduction to This Study Series" (pages 13–14), to stimulate their conversations.

Closing Prayer

Share prayer concerns. Invite participants to pray for their faithful friend and for the group this week and to pray for the meetings in the "Go and Do" portion of the study.

Close with a prayer asking God to support the group's plan for practicing forgiveness in the weeks ahead. Pray that each participant will sense God's support and the encouragement of the group.

Additional Helps

Ideas for "Go and Do"

The idea prompts provided in the study & reflection guide for use in Session 6, "Planning the Next Steps Together" (pages 62–63), should generate many possibilities for what you might "go and do" together. If your group needs help responding to these idea prompts, you can suggest the following:

Lectio Divina Scripture Passages

Plan one or more sessions in which you will explore what Jesus teaches about prayer in Scriptures such as Matthew 6:9-15.

Behavioral Changes to Make

Plan a group session that focuses on the everyday skill of listening. You can ask a pastor or counselor for resources related to active listening skills.

Ministry Events to Consider

Use a session to plan and implement a reconciliation ministry in your church. You can have your group pray for every person in your church throughout the "Go and Do" portion of the study and beyond. Send church members a postcard with Scripture and other quotes about forgiveness and being reconciled. Ask your pastor and the lay leadership of your church to explain your group's study of forgiveness and group members' commitments to praying for reconciliation and peace—in the world, in your church, in individual lives.

Mission Work to Conceive and Implement

Talk with your mission committee about possibilities for mission trips in the United States or abroad in which faith communities are working on the issue of forgiveness and reconciliation.

Speakers to Invite

Invite someone from another church or religious background to come and share her or his perspectives on forgiveness. You might invite someone from the Jewish or Islam faith to speak to your group about forgiveness in their tradition.

Field Trips, Retreats, Pilgrimages to Take

The Fellowship of Reconciliation is the nation's oldest and largest interfaith peace and justice organization. Visit their website for resources, ways to work actively for peace, and fellowship opportunities. Go to *www.forusa.org/*

The Murder Victims' Families for Reconciliation is an organization of family members ravaged by the murder of their loved one. This organization believes, "Reconciliation means accepting you can't undo the murder but you can decide how you want to live afterwards." Your group or your church may have families whose lives have been shattered by murder. Be sensitive to this if you decide to find out more about this group and perhaps become a part of it. They can be contacted at *www.mvfr.org/* or at MVFR, P.O. Box 202875, Austin, TX 78720-2875

Books to Read, Movies to See

"Journey Toward Forgiveness" is a documentary originally aired on ABC television. It tells the stories of people from all walks of life who struggle with forgiveness. It is available on video; the website for the documentary also has stories from the documentary that give practical advice, inspiration, and resources for facing forgiveness issues in your own life. The web address is *http://journeytowardforgiveness.com/*

Read one of the following books. Discuss how the book relates to the Christian trait of forgiveness:

- *No Future Without Forgiveness*, by Archbishop Desmond Tutu (Doubleday, 2000), portrays the unprecedented attempt to heal an entire country, South Africa, after the ravages of apartheid. He explores moving forward with honesty and compassion to build a new world.
- *The Sunflower: On the Possibilities and Limits of Forgiveness* (Shocken Books, 1998) is a rich collection of reflections on forgiveness by prominent theologians, political leaders, psychiatrics, Holocaust survivors, and more. The diversity of opinion and experience makes this an important—and, at the same time, completely accessible—anthology that will evoke good discussion and new insights.
- *Don't Forgive Too Soon: Extending the Two Hands That Heal* (Paulist Press, 1997) takes on the topic of interpersonal violence and forgiveness. Written by Dennis Linn, Sheila Fabricant Linn, and

Matthew Linn, it addresses the classic dilemma of being a Christian: how to stand up for one's rights and be forgiving at the same time. Using both lighthearted examples as well as deadly serious situations, the Linns address the question of turning the other cheek: "Does Jesus want us to get hit again?" This is a good book for a group because it will get people talking.

- *How Can I Forgive? A Study of Forgiveness,* by Joretta L. Marshall, is a study book in the FaithQuestions series published by Abingdon Press (2005). It offers an in-depth study of forgiveness that explores biblical insights, theological insights, forgiveness as a process, forgiving others, forgiving self, forgiving churches and communities, and being a forgiving church in the world. It is written for those who want to live true to the prayer, "Forgive us our sins as we forgive those who sin against us."

Other Ideas

Every aspect of life offers opportunities to practice forgiveness and for being forgiven. Talk with a childhood development specialist. Ask her or him to discuss different stages of "forgiveness readiness." Think about your own childhood and the development of your children or nieces and nephews. How do your experiences and observations stack up to what the childhood specialist says? What correlations do you see between the stages of forgiveness in child development and the "development" of adults you know or have heard about?

A SAMPLE PLAN

Your group might plan a series of weekly meetings in which members would explore and practice forgiveness by reading *Bone to Pick: Of Forgiveness, Reconciliation, Reparations, and Revenge,* by Ellis Cose (Atria Books, 2004). The author explores personal stories of people from "Texas to East Timor," navigating the limits and promises of forgiveness. If you choose this book study option, you might plan a series of sessions structured in a way similar to Sessions 2–5 in the "Come and See" portion of the study, using some or all of the following steps.

Welcome—Greet group members as they arrive.
Psalm and Silence—Choose the psalms you would like to pray.
Look and Listen—Read portions of the study book you choose.
Reflect and Respond—Discuss what you have read.
Lectio Divina—Select Scriptures on the subject of forgiveness.
Pray and Practice—Make assignments for the next session and pray a closing prayer.

Encourage faithful friends to continue to contact one another and to talk about what the group has experienced together.

IDEAS FOR WORSHIP AND CELEBRATION

The final session of the study is a worship and celebration. The group who volunteered during Session 6, "Planning the Next Steps Together," will plan and implement this worship and celebration. Beginning with a meal is a good way to enjoy the friendships developed during this study of the Christian practice of attentiveness. Below are some suggestions to stimulate ideas. You may want to continue such practices as praying a psalm and lectio divina. You also may want to invite your pastor to serve Holy Communion during this worship and celebration. Be sure to make such arrangements ahead of time.

- Create a worship center.
- Share a meal.
- Pray a psalm.
- Sing hymns and praise choruses.
- Create a litany prayer of confession and assurance of God's forgiveness.
- Read the Bible.
- Share testimonies or faith stories.
- Make a commitment to God.
- Celebrate Holy Communion or a love feast.

Gideon testing God
2nd section God testing Gideon
Gideon didn't believe what God
will

Eph 5:17

Gideon dictating God way

Gideon dictated to God
Rather than obey him
knowing what God has to
say about your decision

John 7:17

God testing Gideon
mid 135 000 strong

Renounce all confidence
in yourself and put all faith
in God 2nd cor 4:10
the courag test
Duet 20:1-8 -
comitment test
they were diciplined